CARTOONS OF CYPRUS

ANNE GLYNNIS FAWKES

CARTOONS OF CYPRUS

MOUFFLON PUBLICATIONS LIMITED

Published by Moufflon Publications Limited
20 Costi Palama
Aspelia Buildings, Apartment E1
1096 Lefkosia, Cyprus

publishing@moufflon.com.cy

Copyright © 2001 by Anne Glynnis Fawkes
Drawn on A4 and A3 acid-free paper cartridge paper
220g/m2 with India ink

All rights reserved. No part of this book may be reproduced in any form, or by any means, electronic or mechanical, including photocopying and recording, or by any information storage and retrieval system without permission in writing from the publisher.

ISBN 9963-642-00-4

Designed by George Simonis
Digital manipulation by Simon Simonis
Printed and bound in Cyprus by J.G. Cassoulides & Son Ltd.

Inside front and back cover:
From a complete pictorial map of Cyprus by the author
Drawn in ink for the Artists' Books Exhibition
Moufflon Bookshop, Lefkosia, Cyprus 2000.

Introduction

The cartoons in this volume were done while I was working on a book of paintings of archaeological sites in Cyprus. I had first been drawn to the island by the humour I saw in the ancient artefacts, figurines, models and painted vases, and I hoped, in this more light-hearted collection, to follow the ancient Cypriot artists in producing work of such life and levity. As I researched the artefacts from the sites I was depicting in my paintings, they came alive as characters – the Bronze Age Astarte figurines, Apollo's horsemen and (ironically) the aniconic stone worshipped as Aphrodite at her sanctuary at Kouklia.

Over the centuries, Cyprus's position in the eastern Mediterranean has attracted various peoples who have left an imprint on its archaeology – and in my sketchbooks. The Myceneans and Sea Peoples in particular fired my imagination. Discussions with archaeologists in Cyprus have made me aware of theories and controversies about what happened here, and when – and these have inspired some outrageous scenes in my book.

For an outsider to academic archaeology such as myself, the personalities and interaction of those taking part are among the most interesting aspects of a dig. In some cases this social context can have a considerable influence on the way findings are interpreted. I feel sure that the ancient Cypriots were moved by similar humours and passions.

Although these drawings emerge from some fairly obscure corners of Cypriot archaeology, I hope they will give the reader an enjoyable glimpse of that fascinating, funny world.

Anne Glynnis Fawkes
Lefkosia
January 2001

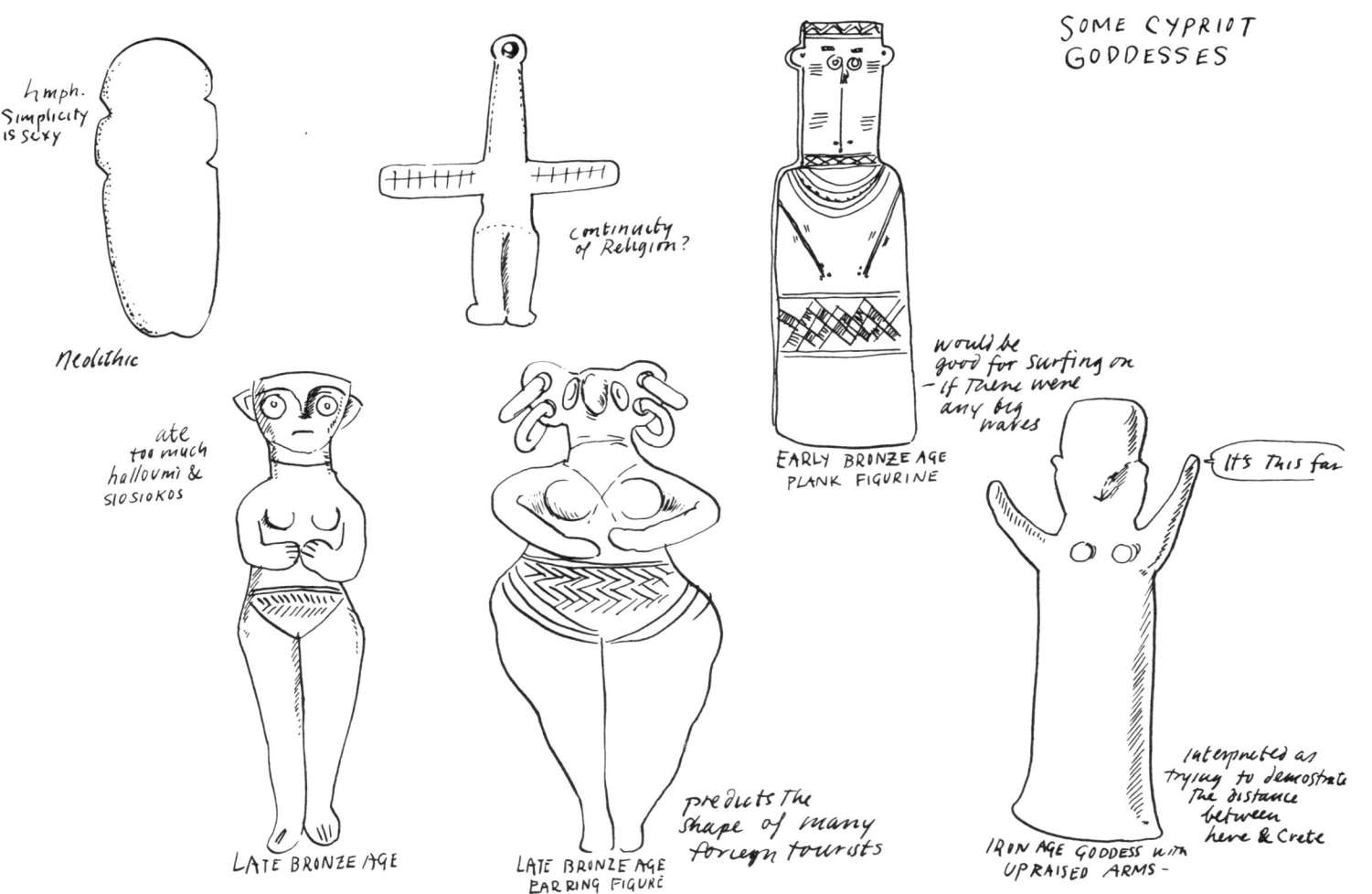

Aphrodite before Aphrodite
First Achaean visitors to Palaepaphos.

The Problem of Reconstructing the Sanctuary of Aphrodite

If Hephaestus married Aphrodite of Paphos

Aphrodite in a Huff

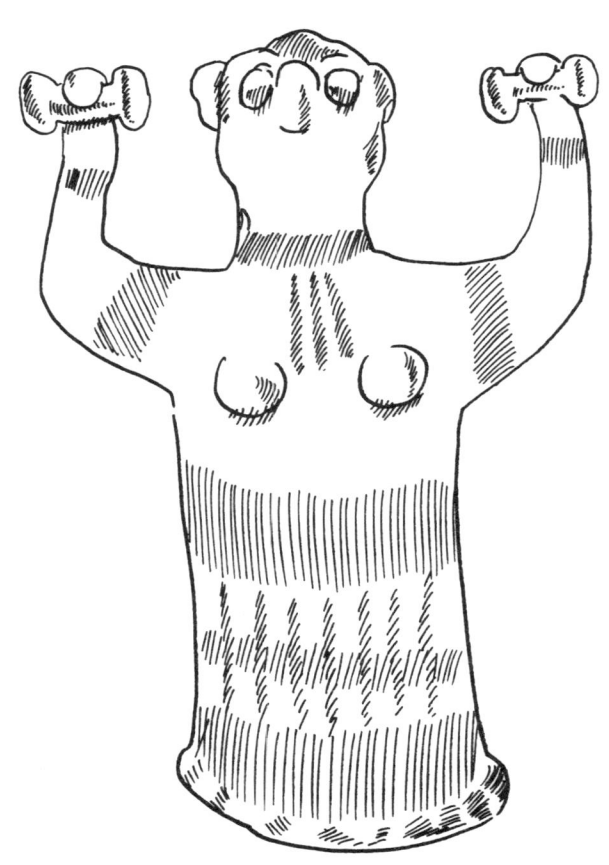

GODDESS WITH UPRAISED ARMS   WORKING ON TRICEPS

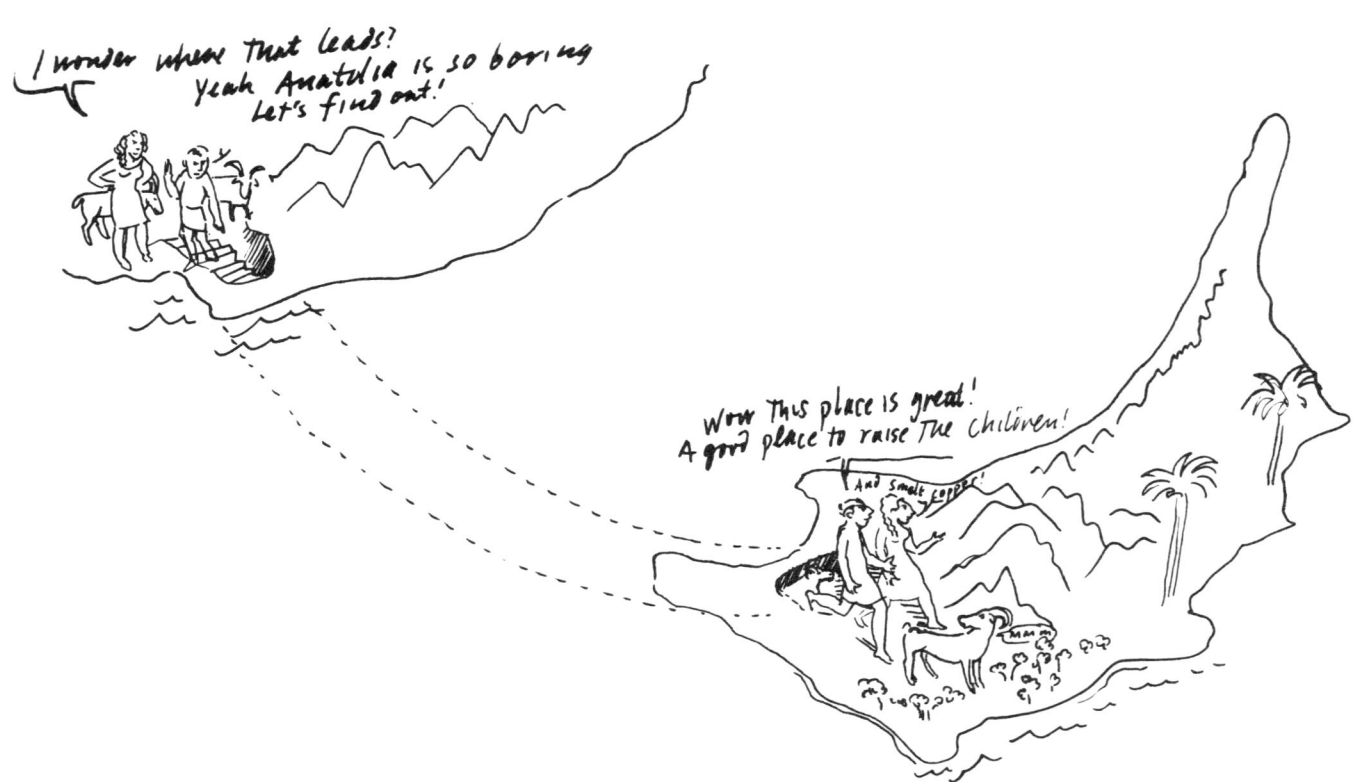

The Latest Accessory — plank figurine cell phone

DONT TEASE the ARCHAEOLOGISTS!

EVERY MORNING OF THE DIG.

Not the time to decide.

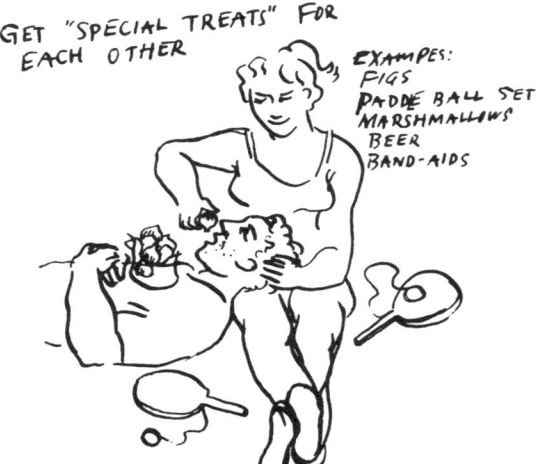

WHERE IDEAS FOR CARTOONS COME FROM

SITE VISITS

WHERE IDEAS FOR CARTOONS COME FROM, cont.

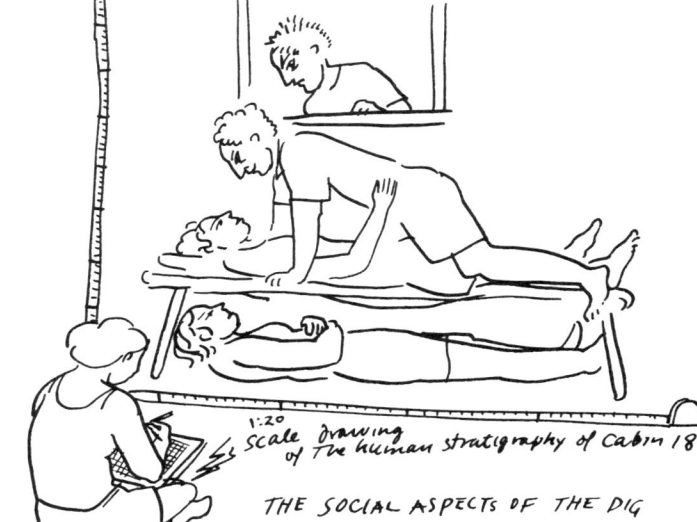

THE SOCIAL ASPECTS OF THE DIG

The hard sell for primo real estate – Kalavassos

The arrival of Horns of Consecration to Cyprus

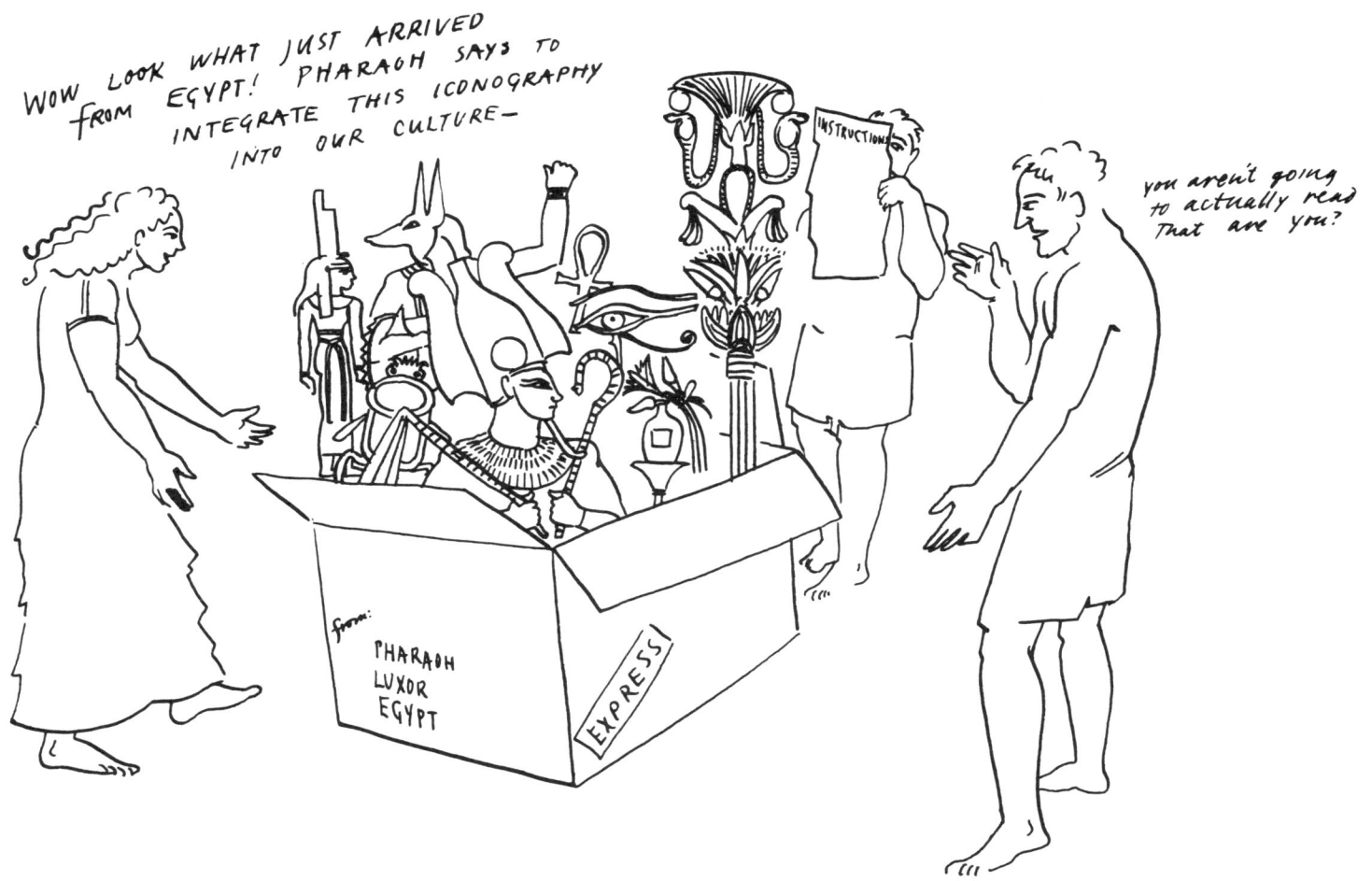

CAN YOU EAT THE ICONOGRAPHY?

ICONOGRAPHY TOURIST

"Nice work on the Ashlars, but my 6-year old could draw better ships!"

CRITICISM of MODERN ART at PHOENICIAN KITION

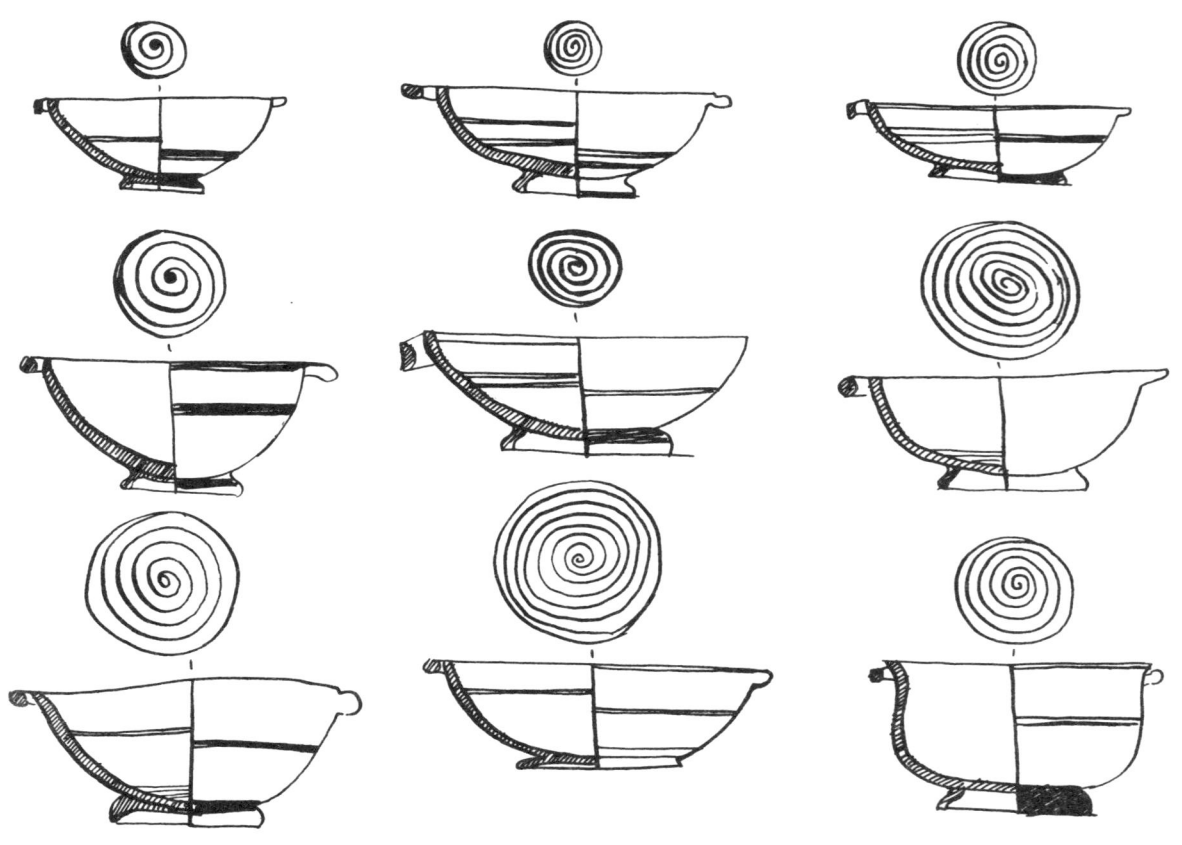

YOU ARE GETTING VERY SLEEPY.... YOU ARE GOING UNDER.... YOU THINK YOU ARE A CHICKEN
The hypnotic effect of the pottery from Tomb 9 (Upper Burial) KITION

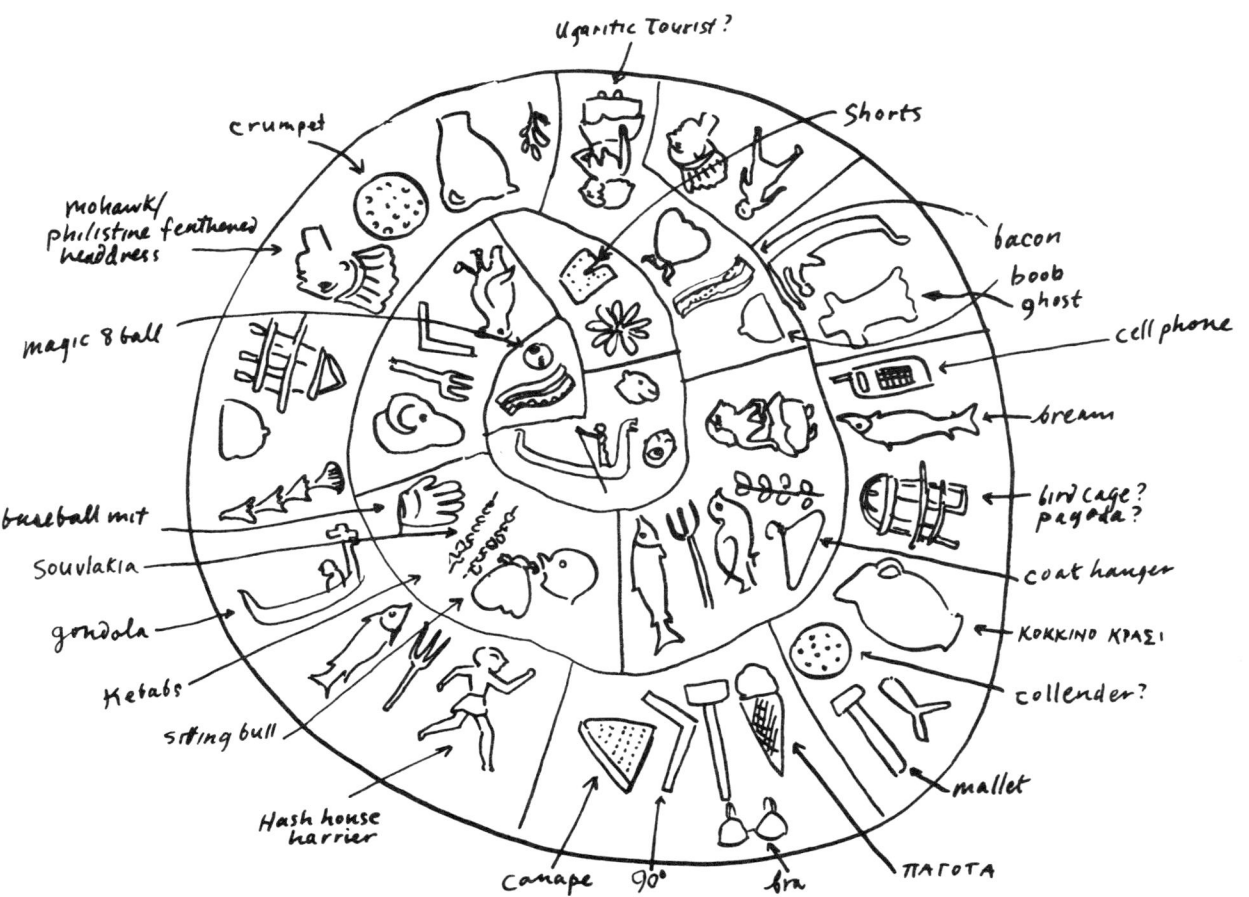

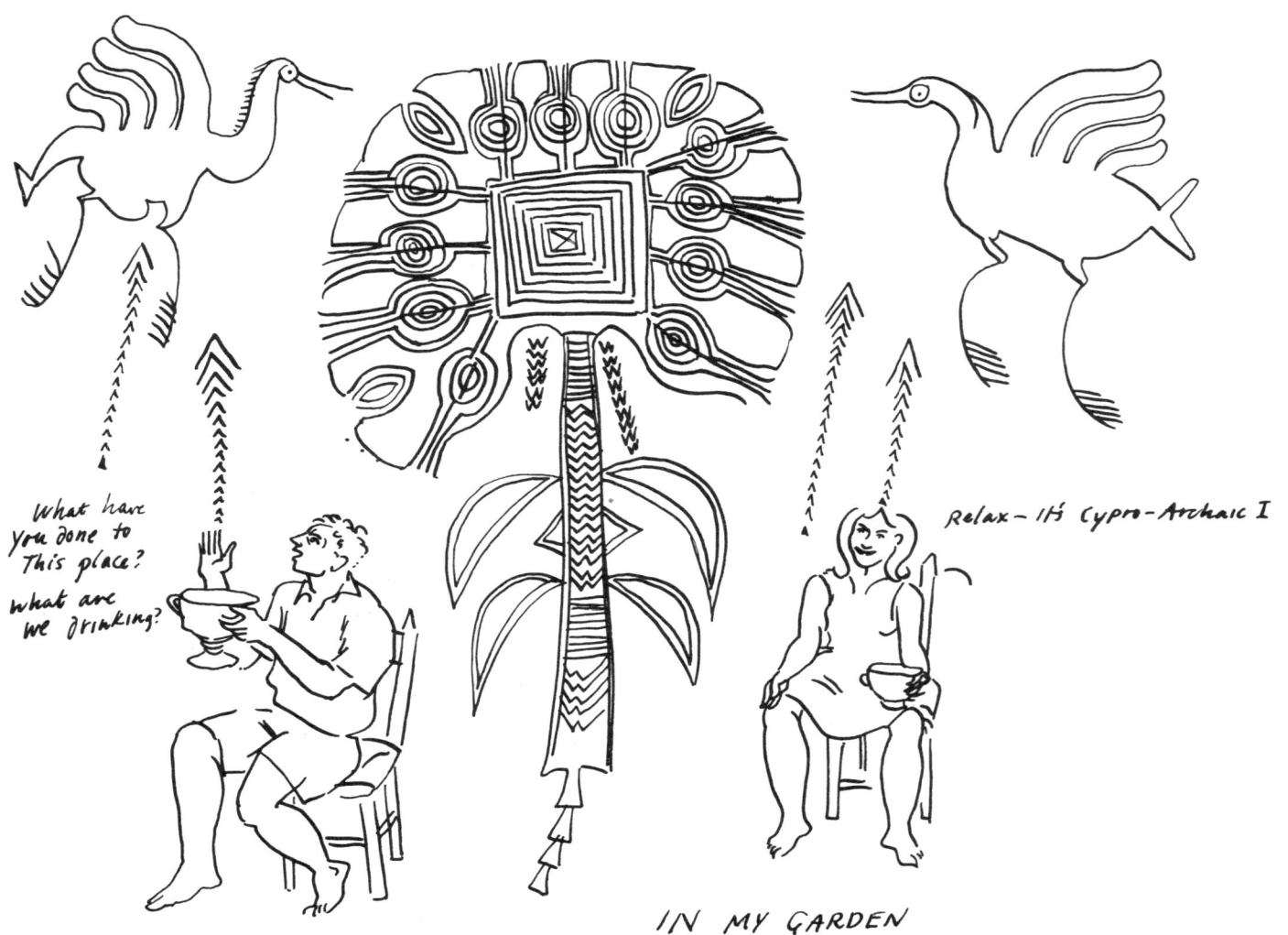

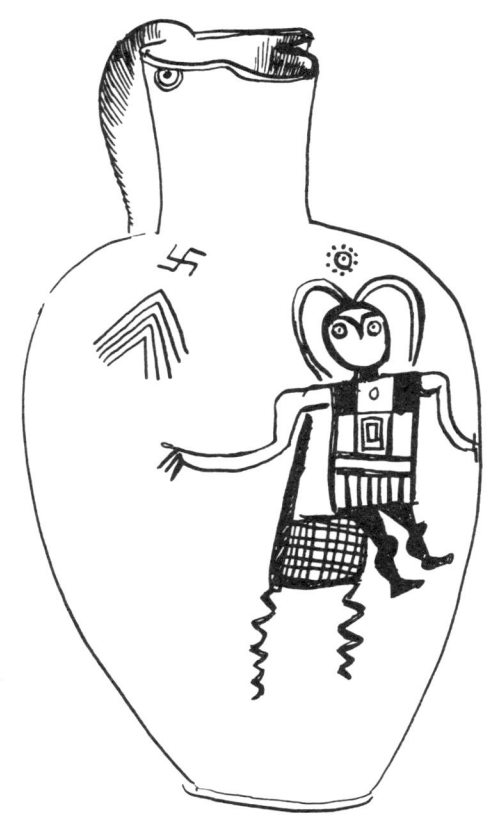 

Revival of The Cypro-Archaic I "Bouncy-Throne"

THE CONNECTIONS BETWEEN METALLURGY, ECONOMY, FERTILITY & RELIGION

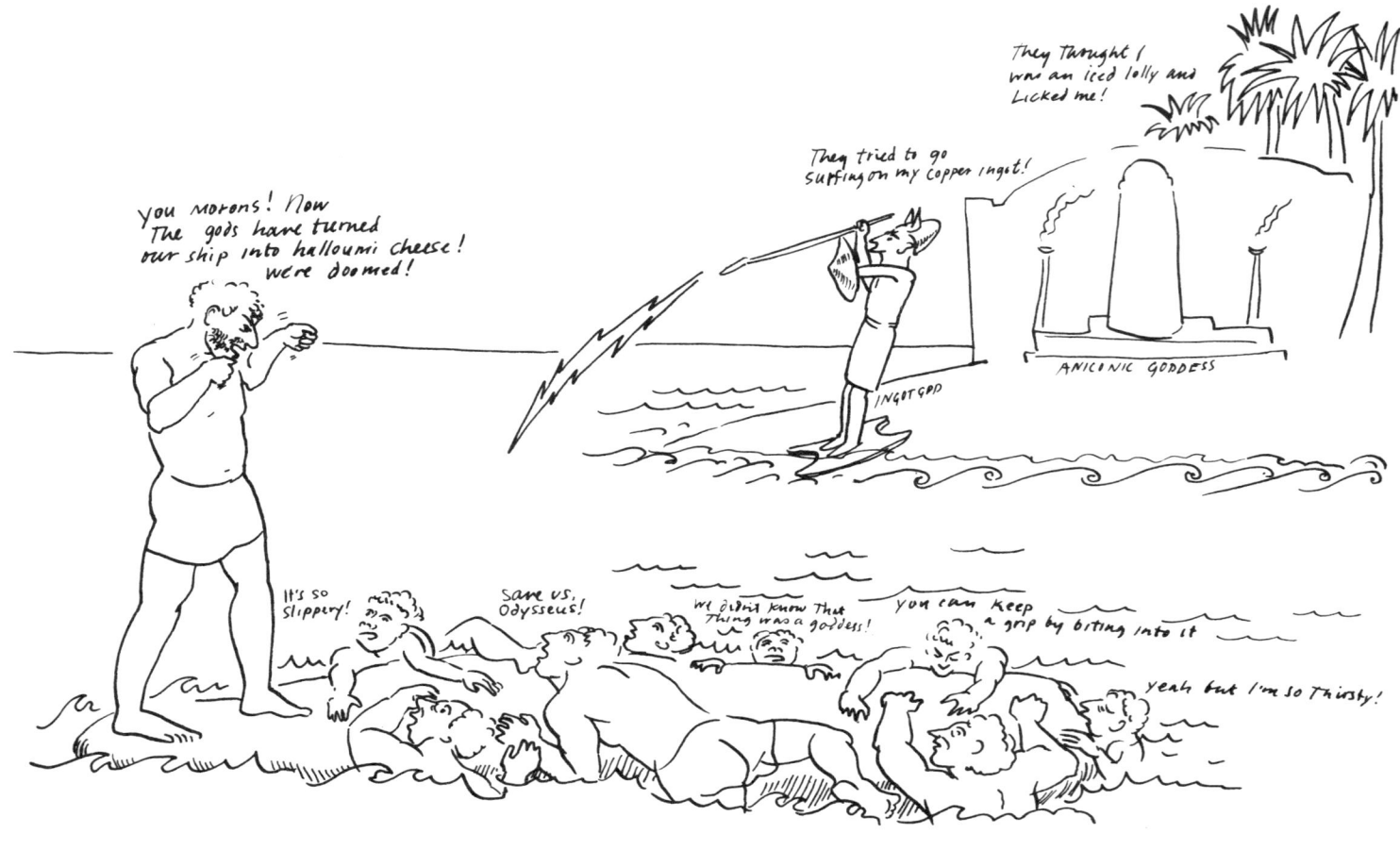

AS USUAL, ODYSSEUS' MEN SHOW A LACK OF CULTURAL SENSITIVITY
FROM A LOST PASSAGE OF THE ODYSSEY — a detour to CYPRUS

THE FATAL GRILL

The 12th c. BC destructions may have been provoked by agressive waiters

Another possible cause of the destructions at the end of the Bronze Age. The Sea Peoples were tired of being snubbed.

The Sea Peoples are entertained in Cyprus

WORK CONTINUES ON THE TEMPLE OF RAMSES II, MEDINET HABU

Again the Chronicle of Cyprus is Interrupted by some Sea peoples

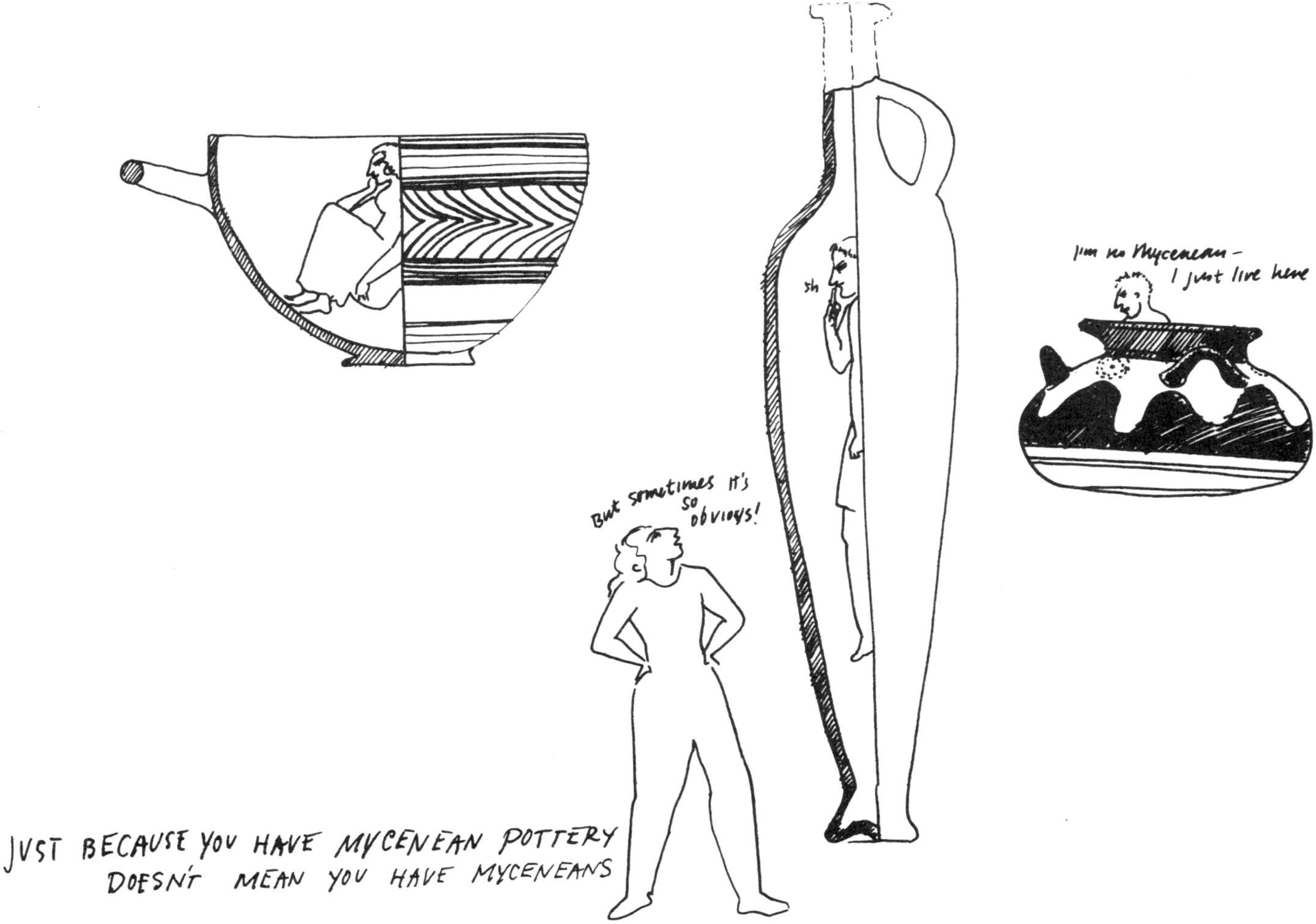

JUST BECAUSE YOU HAVE MYCENEAN POTTERY DOESN'T MEAN YOU HAVE MYCENEANS

"We're going to land soon — now I want you all to remember: They don't know it yet but these people *need* this pottery!"

The appearance of L. Mycenean IIIC — Maa Paleokastro

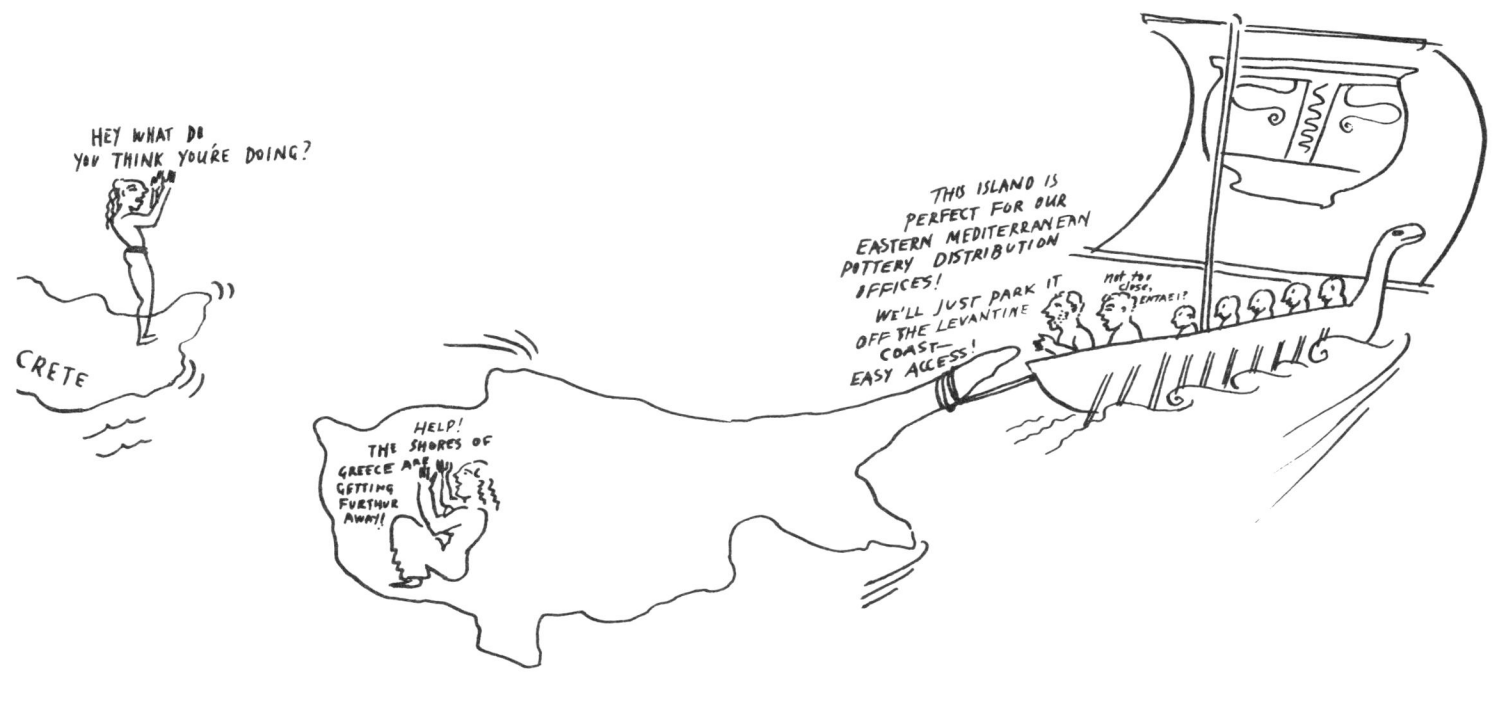

THE GEOGRAPHICAL POSITION OF CYPRUS MAY HAVE BEEN DETERMINED BY THOSE AMBITIOUS MYCENEANS!

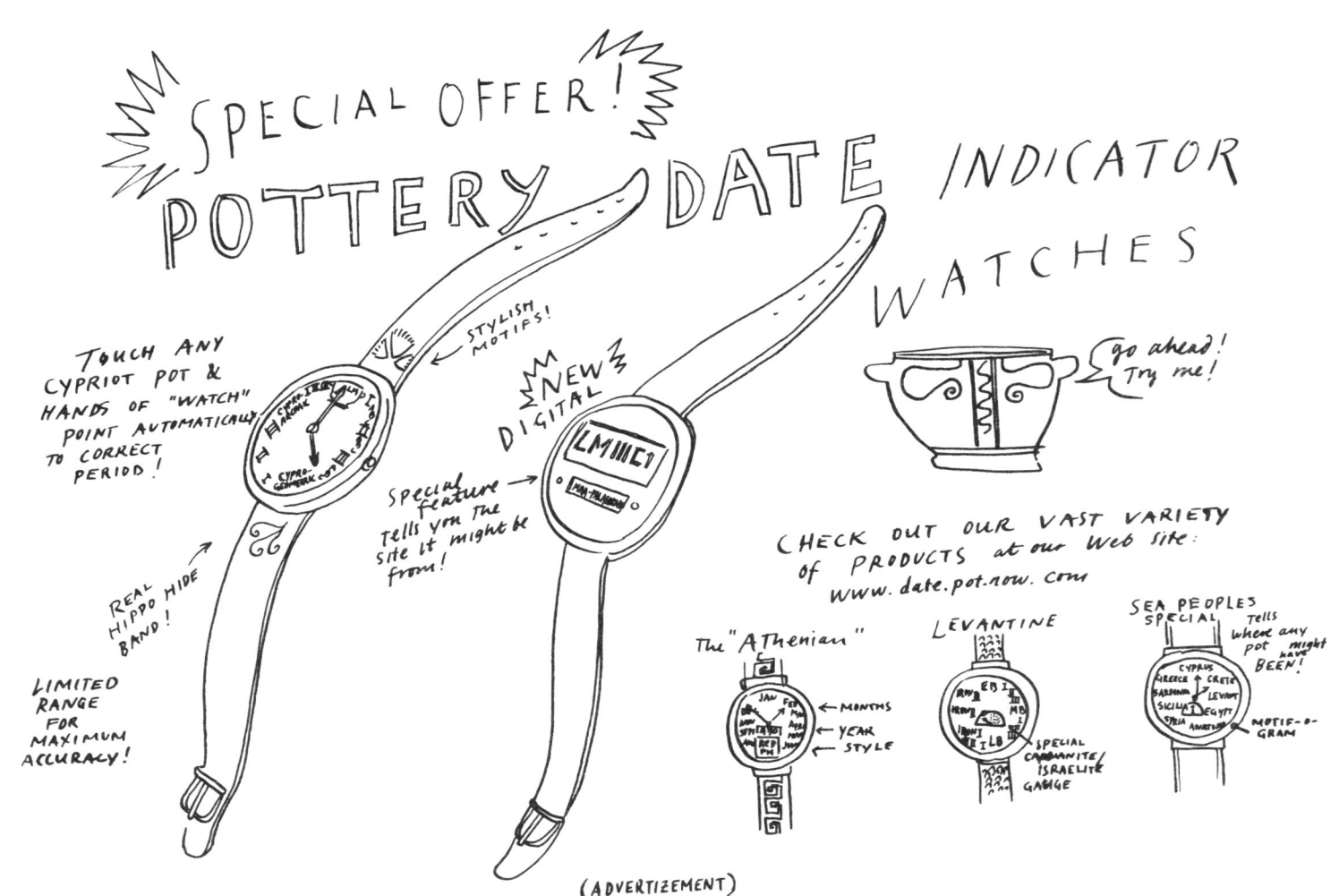

"We don't even understand your obscure pottery jokes — and we're Mycenaeans!"

"I think she faked the design on that LCIIIC krater, eh?"

EARLY BRONZE AGE PARTY-WARE

EARLY BRONZE AGE COAST OF CYPRUS